INITIAL CLUSTERS SOUND EASY!

a phonics **WORKBOOK** for beginning E.S.L. students

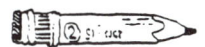

by sharron bassano

illustrated by craig cornell

Alemany Press
a division of
Janus Book Publishers, Inc.
Hayward, California

Copyright © 1983 by Alemany Press, a division of Janus Book Publishers, Inc., 2501 Industrial Parkway West, Hayward, CA 94545. All rights reserved. No part of this book may be reproduced by any means, transmitted, or translated into a machine language without written permission from the publisher.

Printed in the United States of America.

ISBN 0-13-457011-1

0 1 2 3 4 5 D -- P 0 9 8 7 6

Who Is This Book For?

This workbook is created especially for beginning and intermediate adult ESL students of non-academic backgrounds — students who are often mystified by traditional texts, exercise books, and worksheets. Our aim is to provide a medium for listening, speaking, reading, and writing practice of of the 26 most common consonant clusters occurring in the English language in the initial position.

We assume that many of our pictures will be easily identified orally by at least some of your students, and we hope that the illustration style and content are interesting to them. Where the meaning of the illustration is not immediately clear (either to your students or to you), we suggest that you use this occurrence to promote conversation among the class members as you try to clarify what the picture is. Remember that "guesswork" or speculation is a talent we are trying to cultivate in our students to help them cope with ambiguous input often encountered in the creative process of learning a second language. (All answers and intentions *are* given in the back of the text, however!)

In this book, you will not find arrows, charts, or diagrams. There are no detailed instructions, complicated spelling rules, or fine print. We have included only the most basic material for two reasons: 1.) Only you, the teacher, can know the best way to ensure comprehension in your students, based on your knowledge of their background, class experiences, and goals. We leave the instruction up to you and your perception of the students' needs and to your particular teaching style. 2.) We intend that our format will allow spelling rules to be inferred and acquired through the plain, uncluttered pages, thereby eliminating the confusion or anxiety often experienced by semi-literate students who are faced with the printed word. This book is aimed at bringing feelings of immediate success and achievement through its easy-to-follow, consistent format, and hopes to encourage study well beyond this introductory experience.

Initial Clusters Sound Easy! is the third book in our series of phonic/spelling workbooks. The first book, *Consonants Sound Easy,* focuses on introducing the 21 English consonants and the sounds that they most often generate. The second book, *Vowels Sound Easy!,* gives your students recognition of the letters and combinations of letters that generate 11 vowel sounds in English. *Final Clusters Sound Easy!,* the fourth book, assists your students with pronunciation and spelling of over 100 consonant clusters that appear at the end of English words, but that are not commonly found in other languages. Each of these texts allows the students to work with English sounds in simplified listening, speaking, reading and writing activities at the same time that vocabulary is being augmented.

We hope that your students enjoy and profit from using these workbooks; that they experience their beginnings in reading and writing English in a light-hearted, low-stress way. The following pages will suggest a few ways in which you may use this book; however, we invite you to experiment and expand the activities in any way you see helpful or entertaining, using your special brand of creativity and imagination. Please let us know of your success and concerns.

Sharron Bassano
Craig Cornell

How To Use This Book

Name It!

Wherever pictures are presented, allow your students, as a group, to guess at the vocabulary depicted and at the correct spelling. Use this "brainstorm" time to stimulate conversation. Ask them, "Which ones do we already know?" "Who can tell us what number 8 is?" "Does anyone have any ideas about number 14?" "Yes, I think that is right... How shall we spell that one?" etc. As the correct answers are arrived at, write them on the board for all the students to copy in their books. We suggest that as you are writing each word on the board, you give it as much expansion as possible, reminding your students of the contexts in which that item is found. For example, "Yes... that *is* a bru*sh*." "What kind of bru*sh* is it?" "A toothbru*sh*... shoe bru*sh*... oh.. maybe it's a hairbru*sh*." "Do you think it is for bru*sh*ing a dog? I don't know." "Oh, I see... it's for fixing your hair. In the bathroom. Maybe it's on the sink." etc.

When all the pictures on a page have been labeled, you might then dictate definitions or sentences to the class as clues and have them tell you which picture you are referring to. For example: "I'm going to work. I'd better fix my hair..." ("Bru*sh*!") "Boy, is this kitchen floor dirty! ("Wa*sh*!"). If your class is verbal enough, perhaps *they* could give the clues or definitions for each other. Have them make up the context and the answer in pairs, or even have them do the defining or contextualization and *you* guess the word.

Read • Add____

After your students have had the opportunity to relate a particular spelling configuration (cluster) to a visual image for meaning, they are given a chance to read a list of words containing that cluster as a reinforcement of the spelling pattern and to allow for pronunciation practice. Some of the words they will know the meanings of, others, they may not. Tell them that for the moment, meaning is not important. Suggest that they look carefully at the spelling and practice the sound. Have them read along with you in chorus or in small groups for anonymity in practice. Possibly someone may want to try reading the list solo for the class. Also, you might want to pair the students up asking one to read the list in random order while her/his partner points to the words s/he reads. We personally feel no hesitation in assigning *brief* practice sessions of no-sense words (where the meaning is unknown) for the specific purpose of relating and reinforcing a spelling/pronunciation pattern. After reading down the READ list, have the students write in the missing letters — one at a time, pausing to pronounce the change with each word pair. "Rake" (write in B), "Brake", "Rag" (write in B), "Brag" etc. This practice should be brisk! Obviously, where the difference in meaning is not immediately clear, motivation to distinguish and produce the separate sounds is diminished. Keep it short and lively; move about the room during this practice to be sure that everyone is following along.

Listen • Read • Write

These sections may be handled in two ways, depending on your students' proficiency level.

1.) Ask the students to listen to the sentence as you read it and supply the missing word. They will locate the missing word that you have supplied in either the picture section or in the reading list and write it in the space provided. After completing all sentences, have them check their pages with a partner to see if they have both understood and written the same word. Then you might write the correct words on the board for a final check.

2.) If your group is a little more advanced, you might want to have them just work in pairs or threes trying to decide which word from the pictures or reading list would fit in the space and make sense. Then when they have finished, they could correct their pages together as a whole group in consultation with you.

Review Vocabulary

These pages may be handled in several ways:

1. Do as a group brainstorm as suggested for the NAME IT! sections.

or

2. Write all of the correct words on the blackboard but in a scattered or random order. Students work in pairs to decide which words match which pictures and write them in the book.

or

3. More advanced students might simply work together in pairs or threes helping each other remember the labels and the spellings for each picture based on what they studied only.

or

4. You might want to dictate the label for each picture within a sentence, using the page as a spelling and listening comprehension exercise.

Table of Contents

Initial Clusters

page		page	
1	[bl]	20	[dr]
2	[br]	21	[tr]–[dr] Compare
3	[bl]–[br] Compare	22	Review Vocabulary
4	[pl]	23	[θ]–[θr]
5	[pr]	24	Review Vocabulary
6	[pl]–[pr] Compare	25	Review Vocabulary
7	Review Vocabulary	26	[sp]–[spr]–[spl]
8	[cl]	27	[st]–[str]
9	[cr]	28	[sm]–[sn]–[sl]
10	[cl]–[cr] Compare	29	Review Vocabulary
11	[gl]	30	Review Vocabulary
12	[gr]	31	[sk]–[skr]
13	[gl]–[gr] Compare	32	Review Vocabulary
14	Review Vocabulary	33	[š]–[šr]
15	Review Vocabulary	34	Review Vocabulary
16	[fl]	35	Review Vocabulary
17	[fr]	36	Review Vocabulary
18	[fl]–[fr] Compare	37	Review Vocabulary
19	[tr]	38	Review Vocabulary

Initial Clusters

[bl]

Name it!

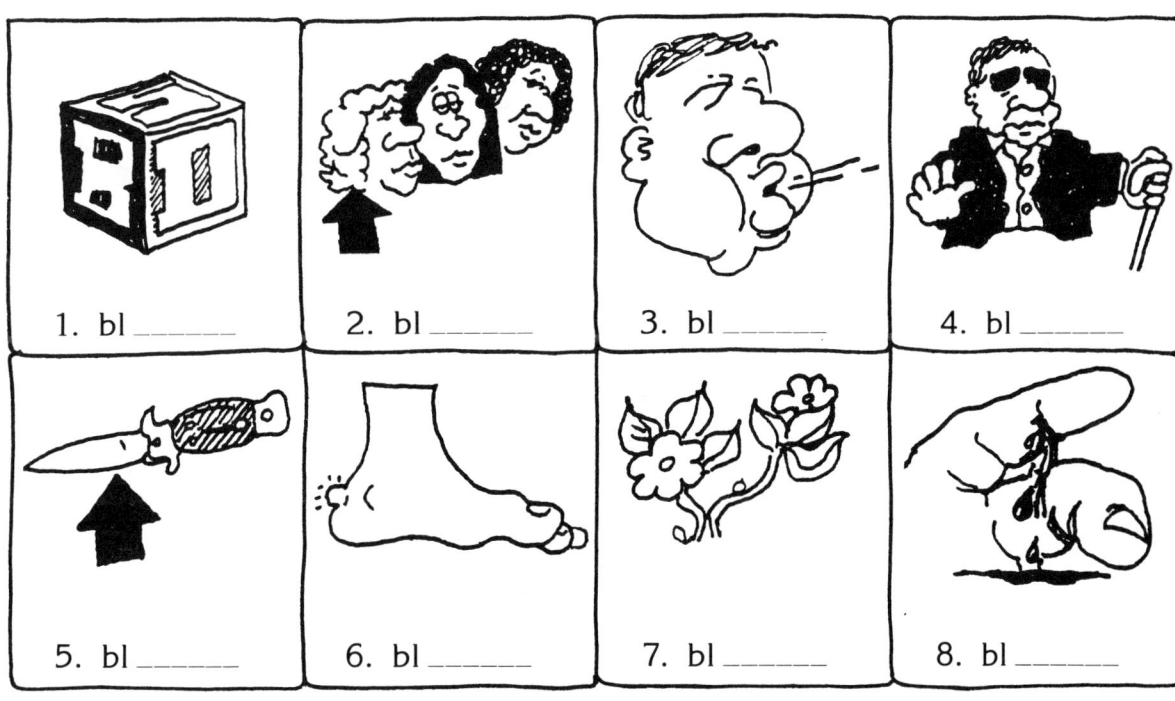

1. bl _____
2. bl _____
3. bl _____
4. bl _____
5. bl _____
6. bl _____
7. bl _____
8. bl _____

Read • Add b

lack	__ lack
leach	__ leach
lend	__ lend
less	__ less
link	__ link
limp	__ limp
lock	__ lock
loom	__ loom
low	__ low

Listen • Write • Read

1. Is that your _____ dog?
2. A _____ is a kind of airplane.
3. My house is one _____ from here.
4. Don't _____ the whistle!
5. Flowers _____ in April.
6. Her hair is _____.
7. My new shoes give me _____.
8. The _____ is broken on my knife.

page 1

[br]

Name it!

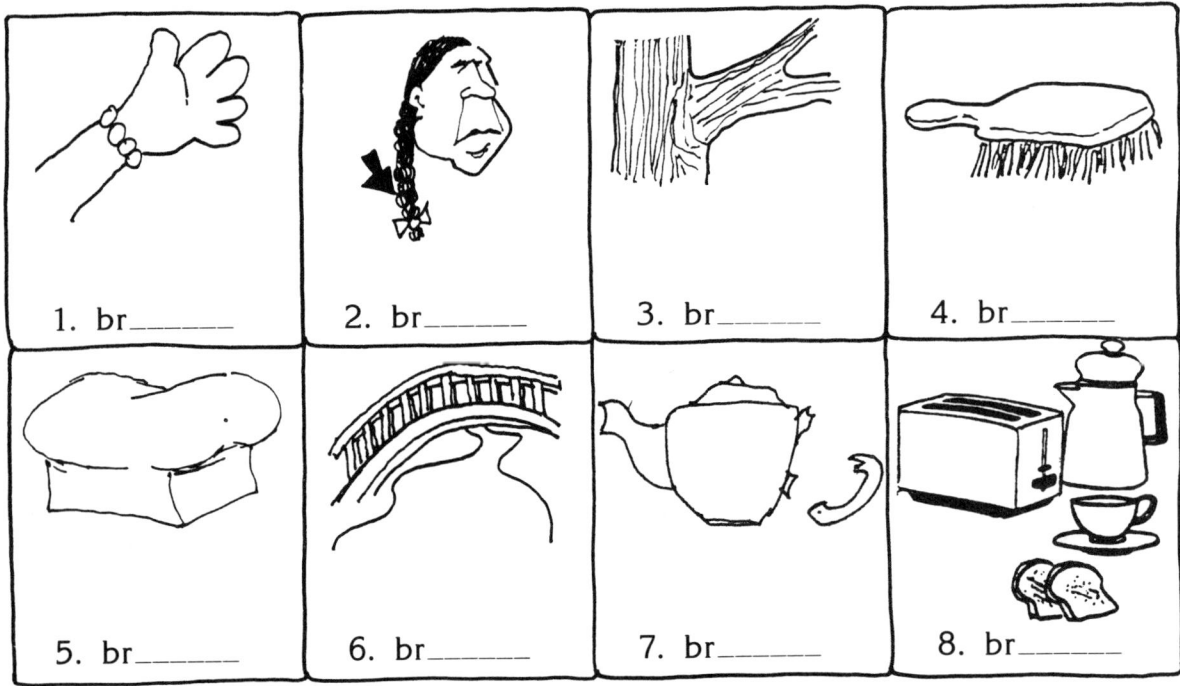

1. br_____
2. br_____
3. br_____
4. br_____
5. br_____
6. br_____
7. br_____
8. br_____

Read • Add b

rake   __ rake

rag   __ rag

ran   __ ran

rain   __ rain

rave   __ rave

right   __ right

ring   __ ring

room   __ room

Listen • Write • Read

1. A _____ woman is not afraid.

2. The sun is very _____ today.

3. Use the _____ to clean the floor.

4. Do you have a comb and _____?

5. A _____ is part of a tree.

6. Some girls _____ their hair.

7. He has a gold _____.

8. _____ and cheese make a good sandwich.

page 2

[bl] [br]

Read   **Add l**   **Add r**

1. bed   b __ ed   b __ ed

2. bead   b __ eed   b __ eed

3. boom   b __ oom   b __ oom

4. bade   b __ ade   b __ aid

Listen • Write bl or br

1. ____ anch   5. ____ oom   9. ____ ed

2. ____ ush   6. ____ anch   10. ____ oom

3. ____ ue   7. ____ ew   11. ____ ade

4. ____ ed   8. ____ ush   12. ____ aid

Listen • Write bl or br

1. A ____ idge is over that river.

2. Where is my hair ____ ush?

3. She likes to ____ aid her hair.

4. Is he a ____ onde or a ____ unette?

5. The ____ anch is ____ oken off the tree.

6. Is this your ____ ue ____ anket ?

page 3

[pl]

Name it!

1. pl _____
2. pl _____
3. pl _____
4. pl _____
5. pl _____
6. pl _____
7. pl _____
8. pl _____

Read • Add _p_

lay   __ lay
lane   __ lane
lug   __ lug
late   __ late
lank   __ lank
lump   __ lump
lace   __ lace
lease   __ lease

Listen • Write • Read

1. Can you _____ cards?
2. The old _____ is broken.
3. She's not very fat. She's _____.
4. Say "_____" and "thank you".
5. They _____ peas in the garden.
6. A _____ is a large feather.
7. A _____ is in the sky.
8. Please put the _____ in the sink.

page 4

[pr]

Name it!

1. pr_____
2. pr_____
3. pr_____
4. pr_____
5. pr_____
6. pr_____
7. pr_____
8. pr_____

Read • Add __p__

raise	__ raise
ray	__ ray
resident	__ resident
rice	__ rice
ride	__ ride
roof	__ roof

Listen • Write • Read

1. Thank you for the birthday _____.
2. That is a _____ office.
3. The son of the king is the _____.
4. If you rob a bank, you go to _____.
5. Don't write your name. Please _____ it.
6. I go to church to _____.
7. What does it cost? What is the _____?
8. His dog is going to win first _____.

page 5

[pl] [pr]

Read   **Add l**   **Add r**

pay   p __ ay   p __ ay

pie   p __ y   p __ y

peasant   p __ easant   p __ esent

Listen • Write pl or pr

1. ____ ank   5. ____ um   9. ____ oblem

2. ____ ow   6. ____ ank   10. ____ ow

3. ____ ay   7. ____ esent   11. ____ actice

4. ____ easant   8. ____ astic   12. ____ aise

Listen • Write pl or pr

1. ____ unes and ____ ums are fruits.

2. He's not going to ____ ay baseball.

3. I need to ____ actice my English!

4. The dishes are made of ____ astic.

5. A farmer has a ____ ow to make a garden.

6. ____ ease sit down.

page 6

Review Vocabulary

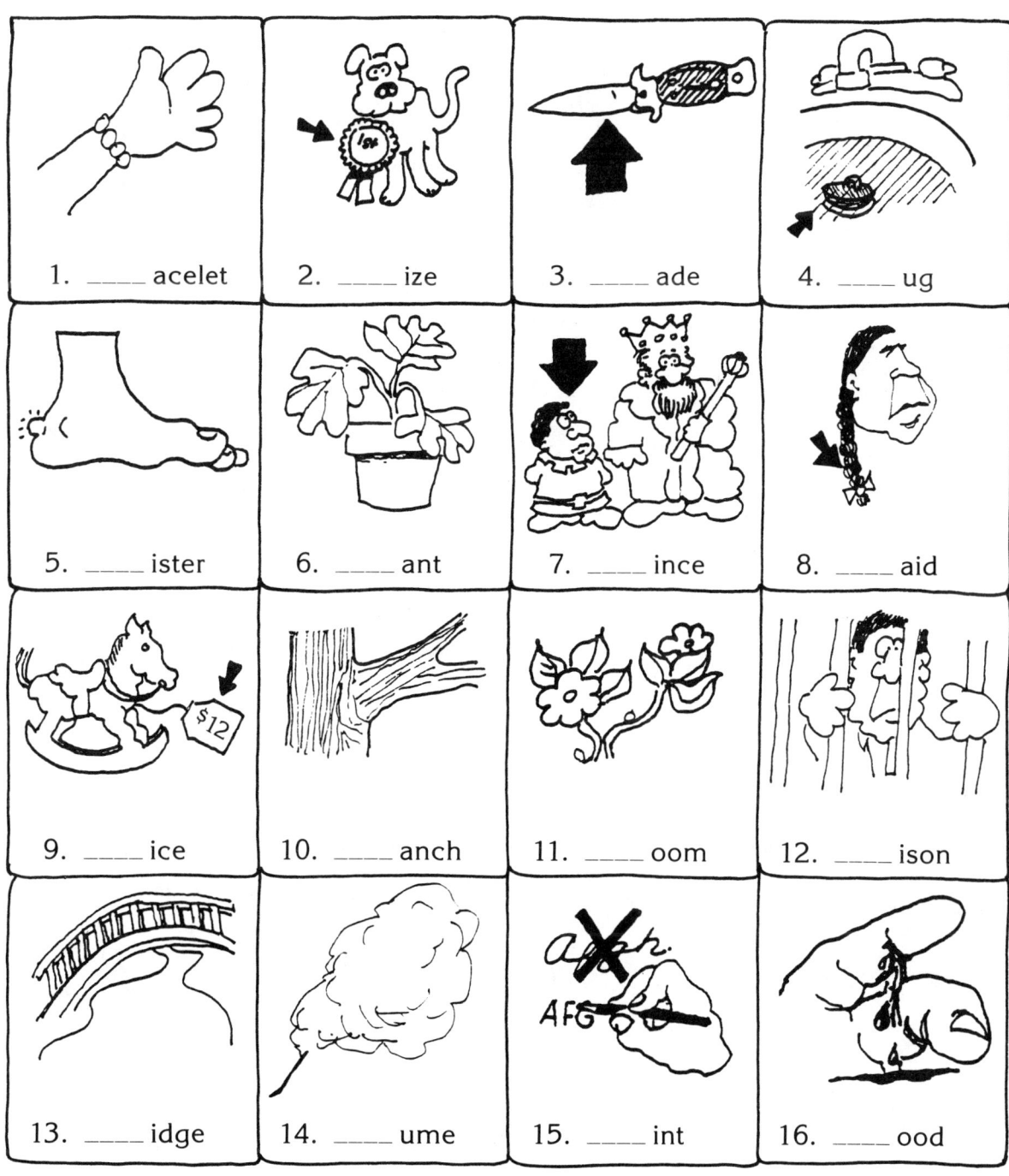

1. ____ acelet
2. ____ ize
3. ____ ade
4. ____ ug
5. ____ ister
6. ____ ant
7. ____ ince
8. ____ aid
9. ____ ice
10. ____ anch
11. ____ oom
12. ____ ison
13. ____ idge
14. ____ ume
15. ____ int
16. ____ ood

[cl]

Name it!

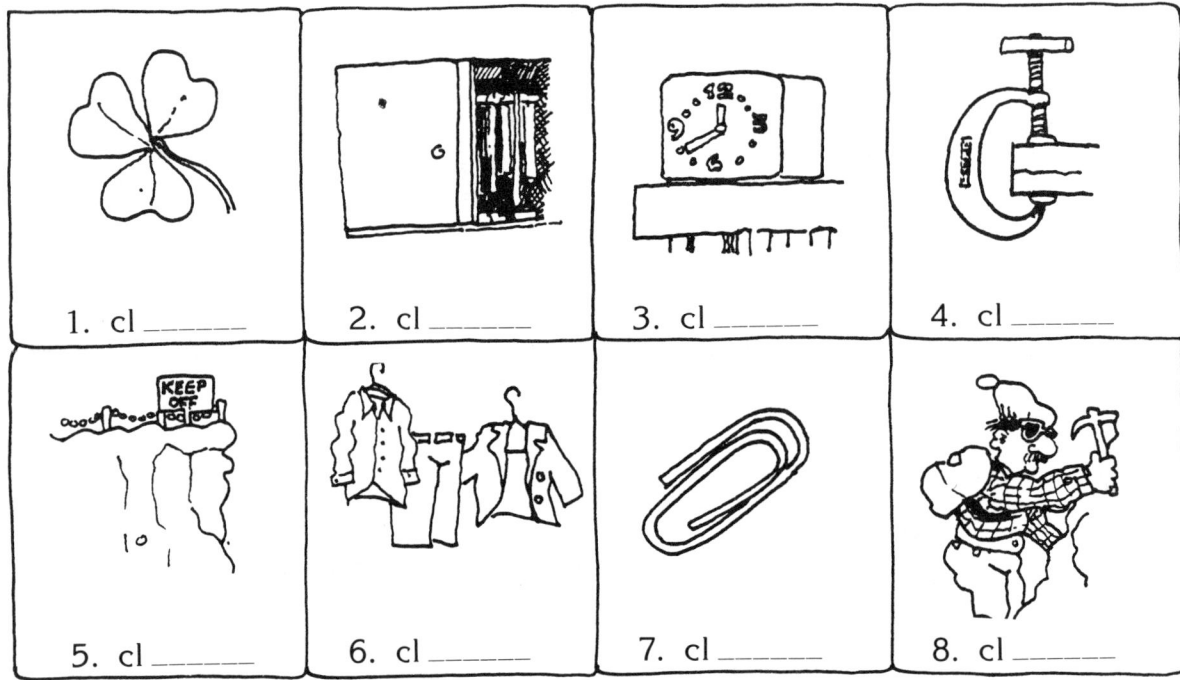

1. cl_____
2. cl_____
3. cl_____
4. cl_____
5. cl_____
6. cl_____
7. cl_____
8. cl_____

**Read • Add c **

lamp	__ lamp
lay	__ lay
lean	__ lean
left	__ left
lever	__ lever
log	__ log
lock	__ lock
lap	__ lap
lash	__ lash

Listen • Write • Read

1. I wash my _____ on Saturday.
2. You shoes are in the _____.
3. A small plant with 3 leaves is a _____.
4. Don't stand next to the _____!
5. What time is it? Look at the _____.
6. The cat likes to _____ a tree.
7. Put a _____ on your papers.
8. A _____ is a tool for fixing things.

[cr]

Name it!

1. cr_____
2. cr_____
3. cr_____
4. cr_____
5. cr_____
6. cr_____
7. cr_____
8. cr_____

Read • Add __c__

rack	__ rack
rash	__ rash
raft	__ raft
rib	__ rib
rock	__ rock
rook	__ rook
row	__ row

Listen • Write • Read

1. Please don't _____.
2. A king's hat is a _____.
3. Children write with _____
4. A _____ lives in the ocean.
5. An insect that sings at night is a _____.
6. A bed for a baby is a _____.
7. The police are looking for the _____.
8. If you need help, call the Red _____.

page 9

[cl]–[cr]

Read	Add l	Add r
1. camp	c __ amp	c __ amp
2. cash	c __ ash	c __ ash
3. cock	c __ ock	c __ ock
4. Coke	c __ oak	c __ oak

Listen • Write cl or cr

1. ____ ack
2. ____ aw
3. ____ ass
4. ____ ock
5. ____ ash
6. ____ ack
7. ____ ouds
8. ____ ass
9. ____ owds
10. ____ ash
11. ____ aw
12. ____ ock

Listen • Write cl or cr

1. We like our English ____ ass.

2. Many people in one place is a ____ owd.

3. You see ____ ouds in the sky when it rains.

4. Finger nails on a cat are ____ aws.

5. A car accident is a ____ ash.

6. A tool for holding 2 things together is a ____ amp.

page 10

[gl]

Name it!

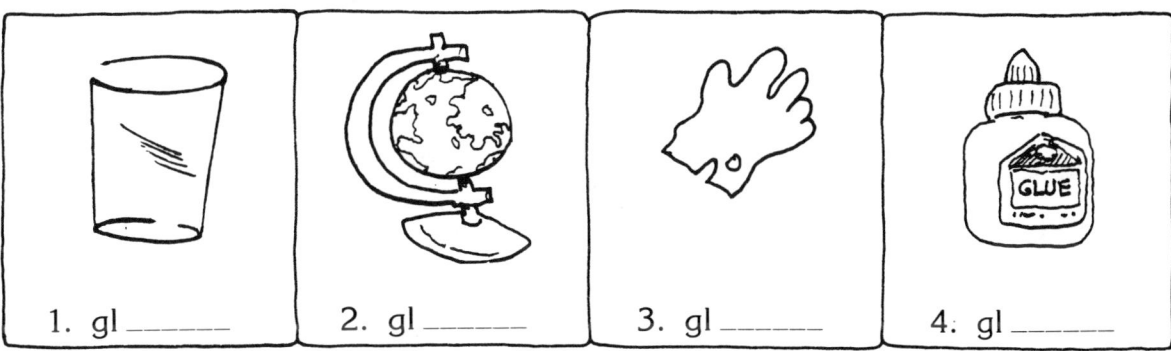

1. gl _____   2. gl _____   3. gl _____   4. gl _____

Read • Add _g_

lad	__ lad
lance	__ lance
lass	__ lass
laze	__ laze
lade	__ lade
litter	__ litter
lobe	__ lobe
loom	__ loom
loss	__ loss
love	__ love

Listen • Write • Read

1. When it is cold, we wear _____.
2. Another word for "happy" is _____.
3. Don't break the _____ please.
4. A _____ is a map of the world.
5. A quick look is a _____.
6. Shiny paint is _____.
7. We use _____ to fix broken things.
8. Some times donuts have a sugar _____.

page 11

[gr]

Name it!

1. gr_____
2. gr_____
3. gr_____
4. gr_____
5. gr_____
6. gr_____
7. gr_____
8. gr_____

Read • Add _g_

rain   __ rain

rave   __ rave

ray   __ ray

raze   __ raze

room   __ room

round   __ round

row   __ row

Listen • Write • Read

1. A _____ is a big smile.
2. Cows and horses eat _____.
3. Bread is made from _____.
4. The _____ brushed the dog.
5. _____ are small purple fruit.
6. Water and sun make flowers _____.
7. My father's mother is my _____.
8. The color of elephants is _____.

[gl]–[gr]

Read	Add l	Add r
gas	g __ ass	g __ ass
gaze	g __ aze	g __ aze
go	g __ ow	g __ ow
goo	g __ ue	g __ ew

Listen • Write gl or gr

1. ____ ass
2. ____ oom
3. ____ ue
4. ____ eam
5. ____ aze
6. ____ ade
7. ____ oom
8. ____ een
9. ____ oss
10. ____ ew
11. ____ ass
12. ____ aze

Listen • Write gl or gr

1. Our children ____ ow quickly.

2. Please give me the bottle of ____ ue.

3. The ____ ass is very ____ een in the park.

4. The lamp is made of ____ ass.

5. Cook the steak on the ____ ill.

6. I have a good ____ ade on my homework paper.

page 13

Review Vocabulary

1. ____ue
2. ____y
3. ____icket
4. ____amp
5. ____over
6. ____own
7. ____andma
8. ____obe
9. ____ass
10. ____oset
11. ____oss
12. ____ain
13. ____ayon
14. ____ass
15. ____in
16. ____iff

Review Vocabulary

1. ____ oom
2. ____ ack
3. ____ ay
4. ____ int
5. ____ own
6. ____ an
7. ____ ush
8. ____ eed
9. ____ ush
10. ____ oom
11. ____ ay
12. ____ an
13. ____ ush
14. ____ int
15. ____ oom
16. ____ ack
17. ____ own
18. ____ ack
19. ____ ate
20. ____ eed
21. ____ own
22. ____ oom
23. ____ ush
24. ____ ay

Name it!

1. _____.
2. _____.
3. _____.
4. _____.
5. _____.
6. _____.
7. _____.
8. _____.

[fl]

Name it!

1. fl _____
2. fl _____
3. fl _____
4. fl _____
5. fl _____
6. fl _____
7. fl _____
8. fl _____

Read • Add __f__

lag   __ lag
lake   __ lake
lame   __ lame
light   __ light
lock   __ lock
lush   __ lush
lunk   __ lunk

Listen • Write • Read

1. The American _____ is red, white and blue.
2. The fire on a candle is a _____.
3. A lamp you carry in your hand is a _____.
4. An insect that likes dogs is a _____.
5. Roses and daisies are _____.
6. A small piece of snow is a _____.
7. A _____ is a musical instrument.
8. Many sheep together is a _____.

page 16

[fr]

Name it!

1. fr_____
2. fr_____
3. fr_____
4. fr_____
5. Fr_____.
6. fr_____
7. fr_____
8. fr_____

Read • Add __r__

fame	f__ ame
fee	f__ ee
fend	f__ iend
fog	f__ og
fight	f__ ight

Listen • Write • Read

1. We cook eggs in a _____ .
2. The students are good _____.
3. He has _____ on his nose.
4. Mr. DuFils is from _____.
5. Bananas and apples are _____.
6. A little green animal is a _____.
7. If it has no price, it is _____.
8. Around the picture is a _____.

Read	Add __l__	Add __r__
fame	f __ ame	f __ ame
fee	f __ ee	f __ ee
fight	f __ ight	f __ ight
food	f __ ute	f __ uit

Listen • Write __fl__ or __fr__

1. ____ esh
2. ____ ank
3. ____ ight
4. ____ uit
5. ____ ame
6. ____ ight
7. ____ esh
8. ____ eezer
9. ____ ank
10. ____ ute
11. ____ eight
12. ____ ont

Listen • Write __fl__ or __fr__

1. Is this fish ____ esh?
2. What kind of ____ uit do you like?
3. Put the ice cream in the ____ eezer.
4. Can she play the ____ ute?
5. Don't sit in back. Sit in ____ ont.
6. The tickets are ____ ee!

Name it!

[tr]

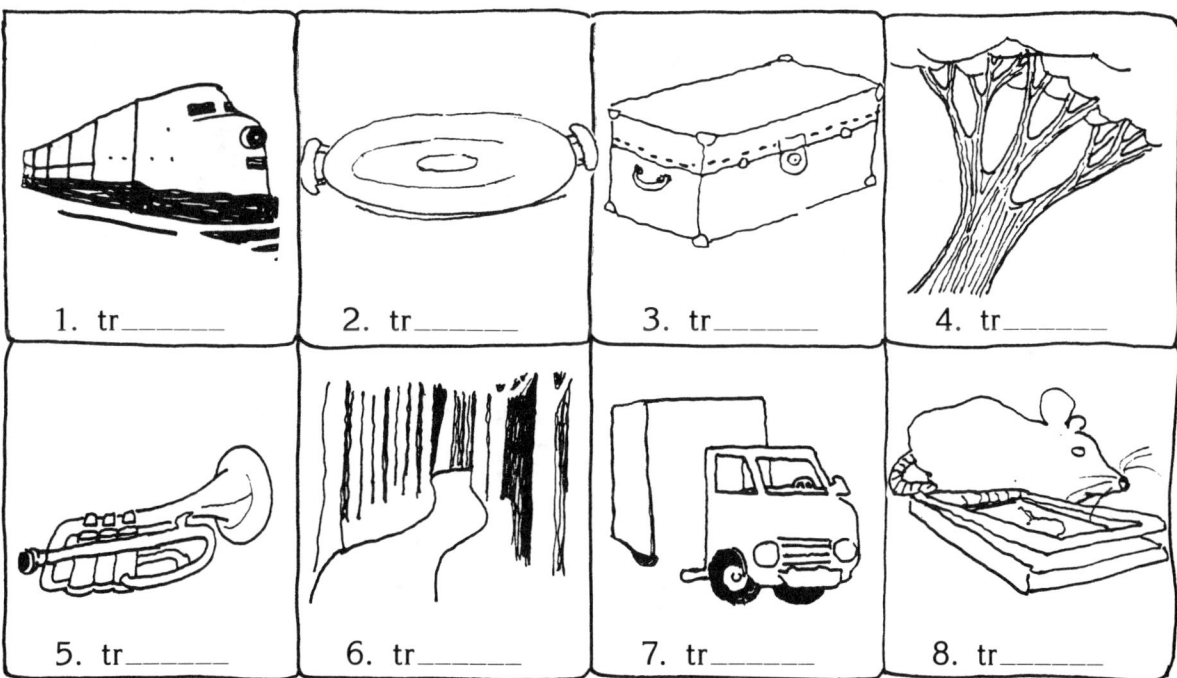

1. tr_____
2. tr_____
3. tr_____
4. tr_____
5. tr_____
6. tr_____
7. tr_____
8. tr_____

Read • Add __t__

rain	__ rain
ray	__ ray
rap	__ rap
red	__ read
rip	__ rip

Listen • Write • Read

1. A pine is a kind of _____.
2. A pick-up is a kind of _____.
3. A _____ is slower than an airplane.
4. Serve the lunch on a _____.
5. The mouse is in the _____.
6. Put the blankets in the _____.
7. _____ and guitars are musical instruments.
8. In the mountains we walk on a _____.

[dr]

Name it!

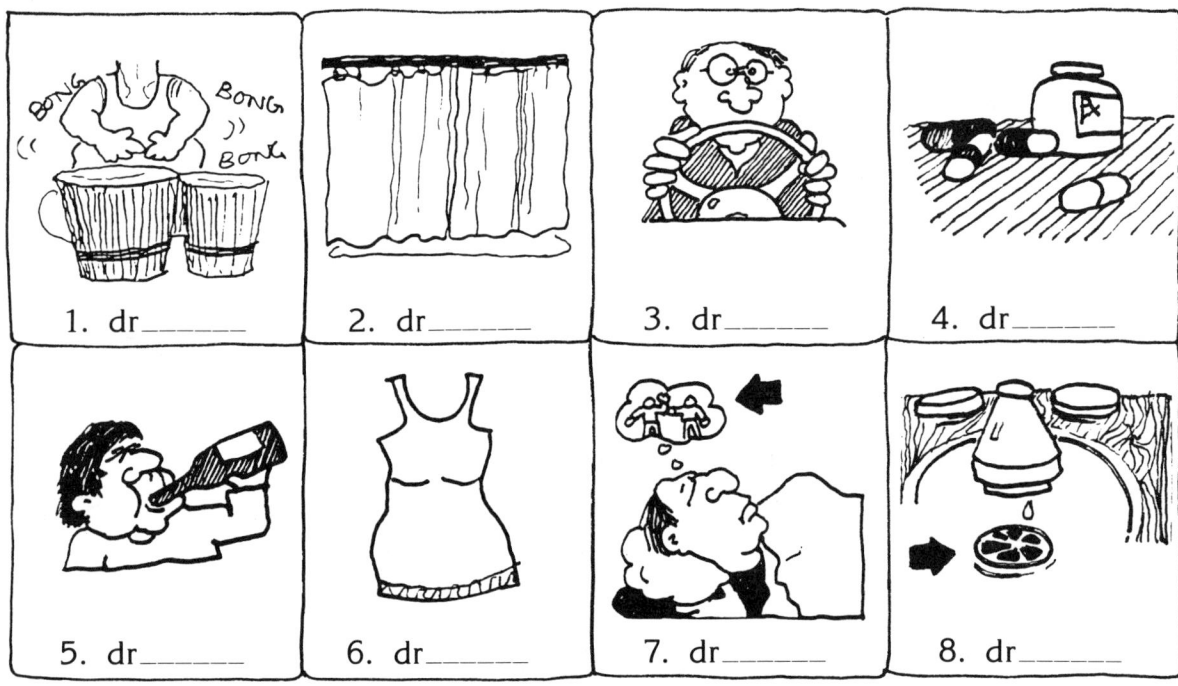

1. dr_____
2. dr_____
3. dr_____
4. dr_____
5. dr_____
6. dr_____
7. dr_____
8. dr_____

Read • Add d

rain	__ rain
rum	__ rum
rink	__ rink
rag	__ rag
raw	__ raw
rift	__ rift
rip	__ rip
rugs	__ rugs

Listen • Write • Read

1. A woman wears a _____.
2. Coffee is a hot _____.
3. A _____ is a musical instrument.
4. I _____ when I sleep.
5. Penicillin is a _____.
6. Can you _____ a car?
7. _____ are long curtains
8. Water in the sink goes down the _____.

[tr] [dr]

Read   **Add d**   **Add t**

rain   ____ rain   ____ rain
rill   ____ rill   ____ rill
red   ____ read   ____ read

Listen • Write dr or tr

1. ____ ail   5. ____ ess   9. ____ ip
2. ____ uck   6. ____ ue   10. ____ ip
3. ____ y   7. ____ y   11. ____ ink
4. ____ ee   8. ____ op   12. ____ apes

Listen • Write dr or tr

1. An apple ____ ee is in front of my house.
2. Can you ____ ive a ____ uck?
3. I'm taking a ____ ain to Los Angeles.
4. ____ y your hands on the towel.
5. She's wearing a new red ____ ess.
6. Please ____ aw me a picture of a horse.

page 21

Review Vocabulary

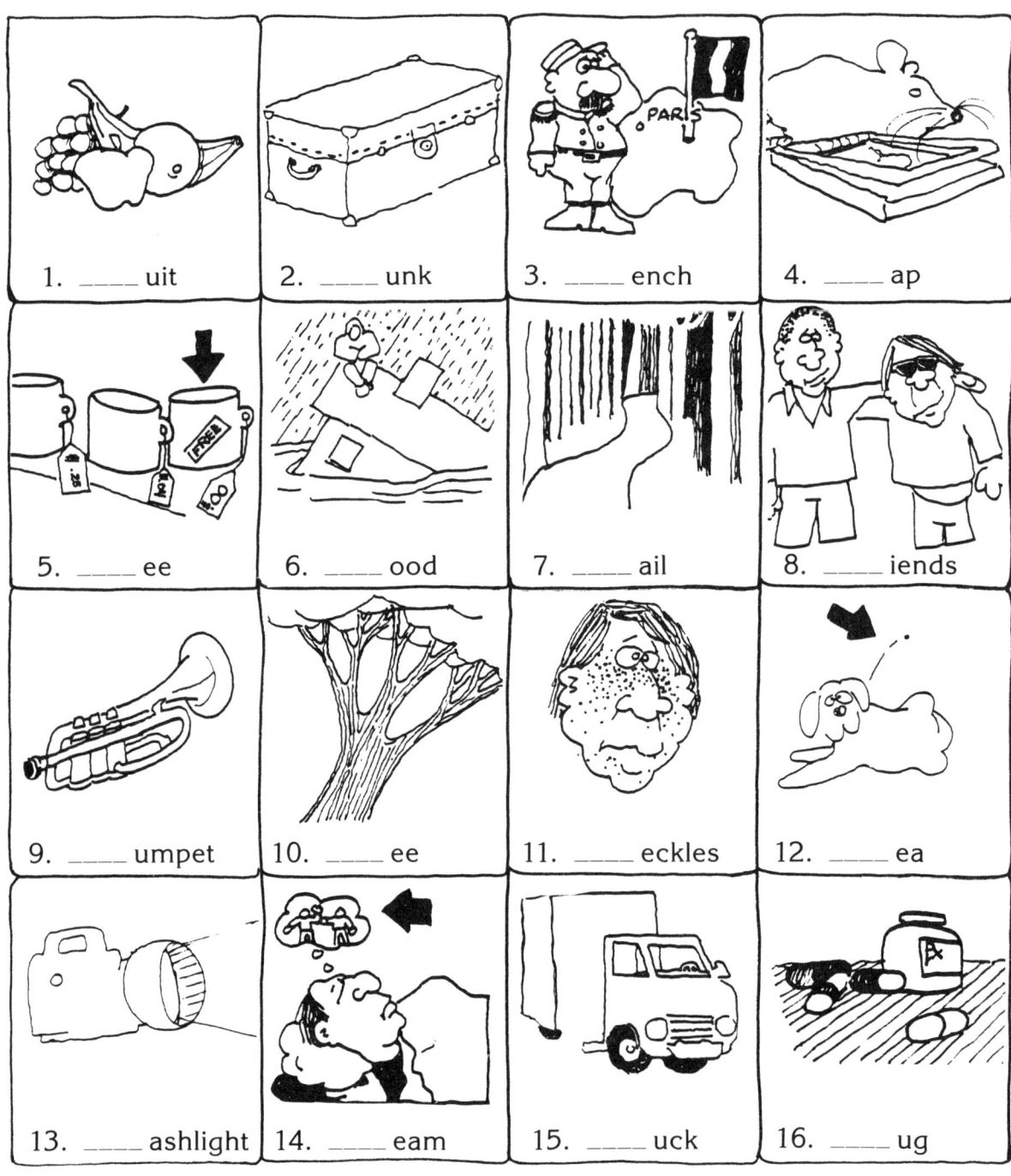

1. ____ uit
2. ____ unk
3. ____ ench
4. ____ ap
5. ____ ee
6. ____ ood
7. ____ ail
8. ____ iends
9. ____ umpet
10. ____ ee
11. ____ eckles
12. ____ ea
13. ____ ashlight
14. ____ eam
15. ____ uck
16. ____ ug

[θ]–[θr]

Name it!

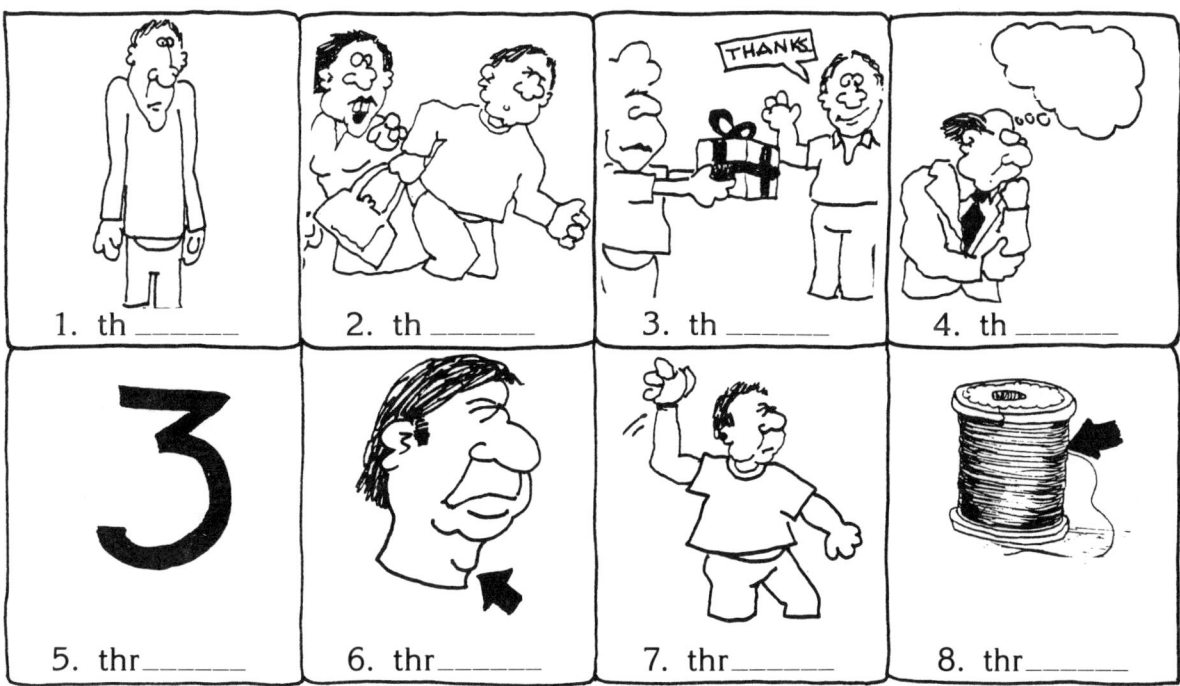

1. th_____
2. th_____
3. th_____
4. th_____
5. thr_____
6. thr_____
7. thr_____
8. thr_____

Listen • Write • Read

1. If you want to sew on a button you need _____.

2. He's not fat. He's _____.

3. Susan has _____ sisters.

4. Do you _____ about your family?

5. I want to say "_____ you" for the present.

6. _____ the ball to me!

7. I have a cold. My _____ is sore.

8. The _____ took the money from the bank.

Review Vocabulary

1. ____ ain
2. ____ iends
3. ____ ame
4. ____ um
5. ____ in
6. ____ uck
7. ____ og
8. ____ ead
9. ____ ue
10. ____ aw
11. ____ ink
12. ____ uit
13. ____ uck
14. ____ ute
15. ____ ink
16. ____ oat
17. ____ ee
18. ____ ag
19. ____ ay
20. ____ ame
21. ____ esser
22. ____ ip
23. ____ y
24. ____ ief

Name it!

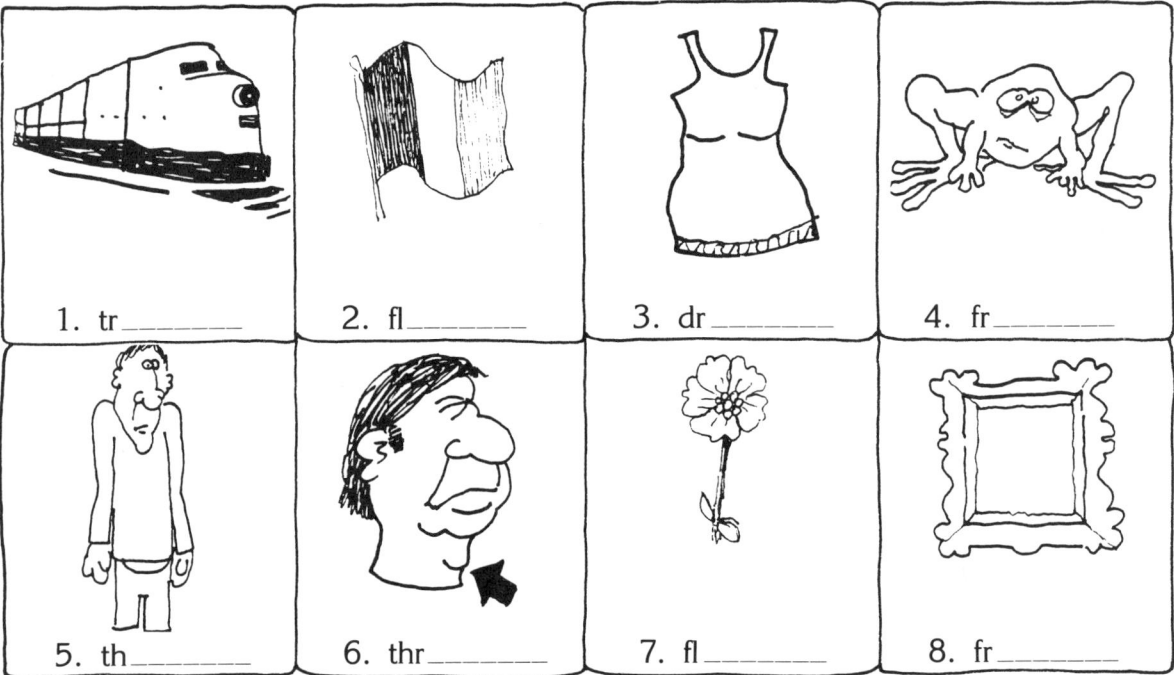

1. tr_____
2. fl_____
3. dr_____
4. fr_____
5. th_____
6. thr_____
7. fl_____
8. fr_____

Review Vocabulary

1. _____ ivate
2. _____ ate
3. _____ ond
4. _____ othes
5. _____ ay
6. _____ ay
7. _____ ying pan
8. _____ ab
9. _____ ive
10. _____ ind
11. _____ ay
12. _____ um
13. _____ oom
14. _____ ip
15. _____ ain
16. _____ ook

Name it! [sp] [spr] [spl]

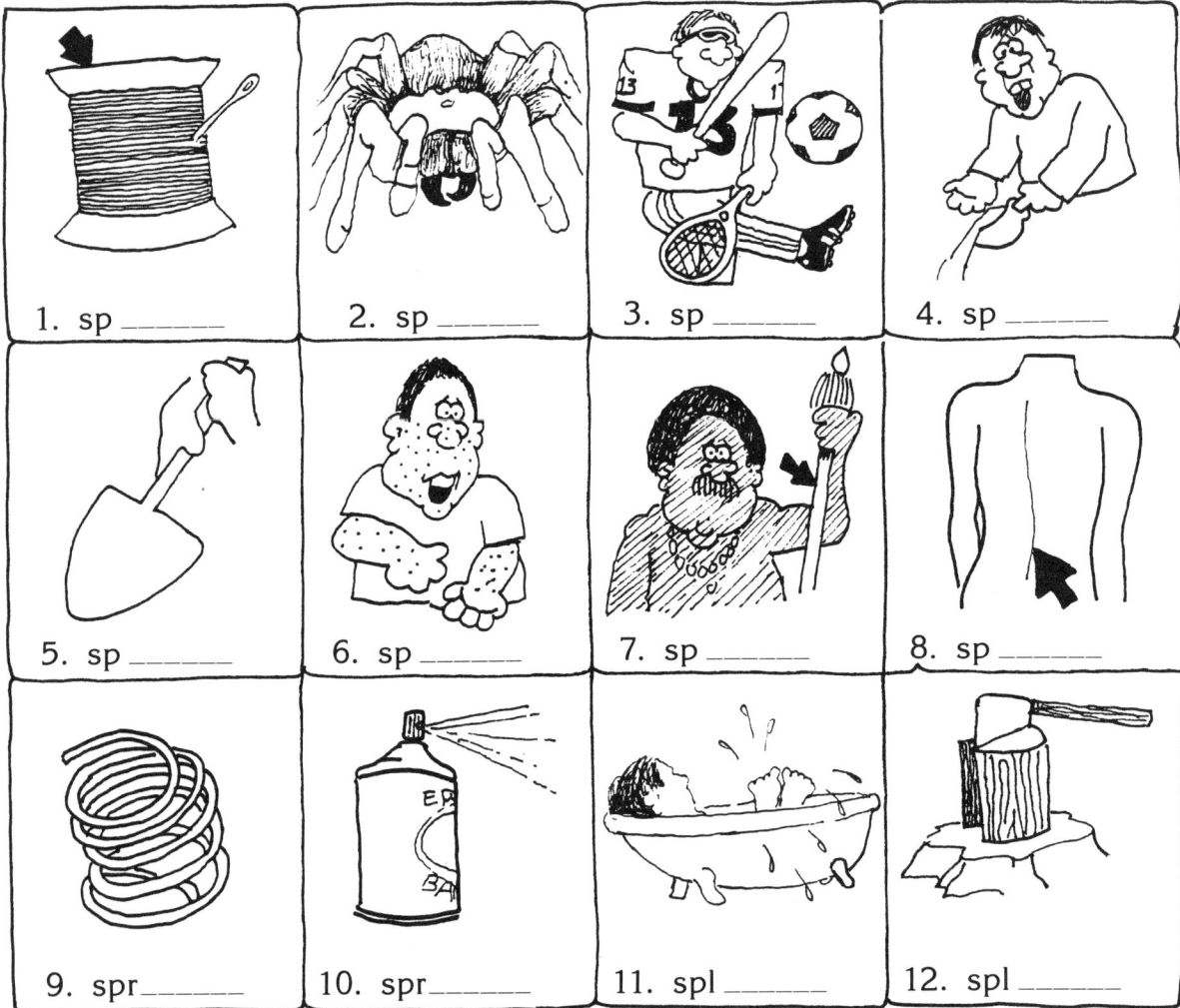

1. sp _____
2. sp _____
3. sp _____
4. sp _____
5. sp _____
6. sp _____
7. sp _____
8. sp _____
9. spr _____
10. spr _____
11. spl _____
12. spl _____

Read • Add sp

ray	____ ray
ring	____ ring
rocket	____ rocket
lash	____ lash
lit	____ lit
latter	____ latter
end	____ end
it	____ it
oil	____ oil

Listen • Write • Read

1. I need a _____ of black thread.
2. Baseball and tennis are _____.
3. I'm afraid of _____.
4. Please don't _____ the milk.
5. _____ the garden with the hose.
6. Babies like to _____ in the bath.
7. A leopard has _____.
8. I always _____ to much money at the market.

Name it!

[st] [str]

Read

seam	steam	stream
sand	stand	strand
sing	sting	string

Listen • Write • Read

1. Do you have an airmail _____.
2. A _____ is a small river.
3. I ate too much. My _____ hurts.
4. The _____ on my kite is broken.
5. The _____ are beautiful tonight.
6. Hot water makes _____.
7. Are you a new _____?
8. Musicians _____ on a _____.

Name it!

[sm] [sn] [sl]

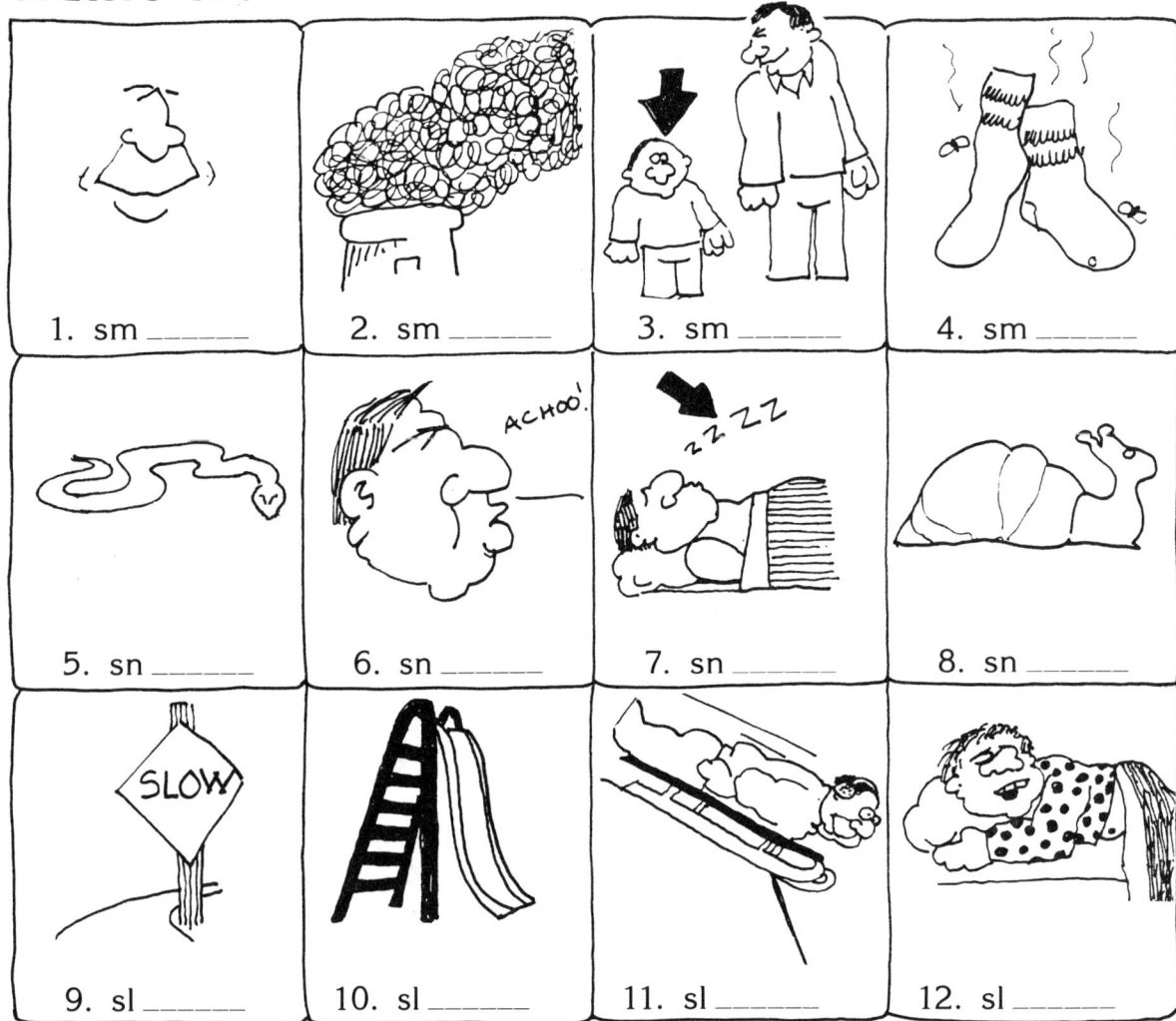

1. sm _____
2. sm _____
3. sm _____
4. sm _____
5. sn _____
6. sn _____
7. sn _____
8. sn _____
9. sl _____
10. sl _____
11. sl _____
12. sl _____

Read • Add _s_

mash	__ mash
mile	__ mile
mall	__ mall
lap	__ lap
lender	__ lender
low	__ low
nap	__ nap
nail	__ nail

Listen • Write • Read

1. Do you _____ _____?
2. A _____ is very _____.
3. Does your husband _____?
4. Don't be sad. _____!
5. Is that your _____ dog?
6. Children like to play on a _____.
7. Do you see that _____?
8. When you have a cold, you _____.

Review

1. spring	2. speak	3. spay	4. spy	5. splash
sting	streak	stray	sty	stash
string	sneak	spray	spry	smash
sling	sleek	stay	sly	slash

Listen • Write • Read

1. Do you _____ eak Chinese?
2. She doesn't buy hair _____ ay.
3. A bee _____ ing hurts!
4. I want four _____ all cookies, please.
5. I need some _____ ing for my kite.
6. He's wearing a _____ aw hat.
7. Does it _____ ow in California?
8. Take a taxi. The bus is too _____ ow.
9. Where are you going to _____ ay?
10. Look out! There's a _____ ake!!

page 29

Review Vocabulary

1. ____ ool
2. ____ all
3. ____ amp
4. ____ aw
5. ____ ike
6. ____ ing
7. ____ ore
8. ____ orts
9. ____ ing
10. ____ ash
11. ____ ow
12. ____ oke
13. ____ ake
14. ____ eeze
15. ____ ove
16. ____ ay

Name it! [sk] [skr]

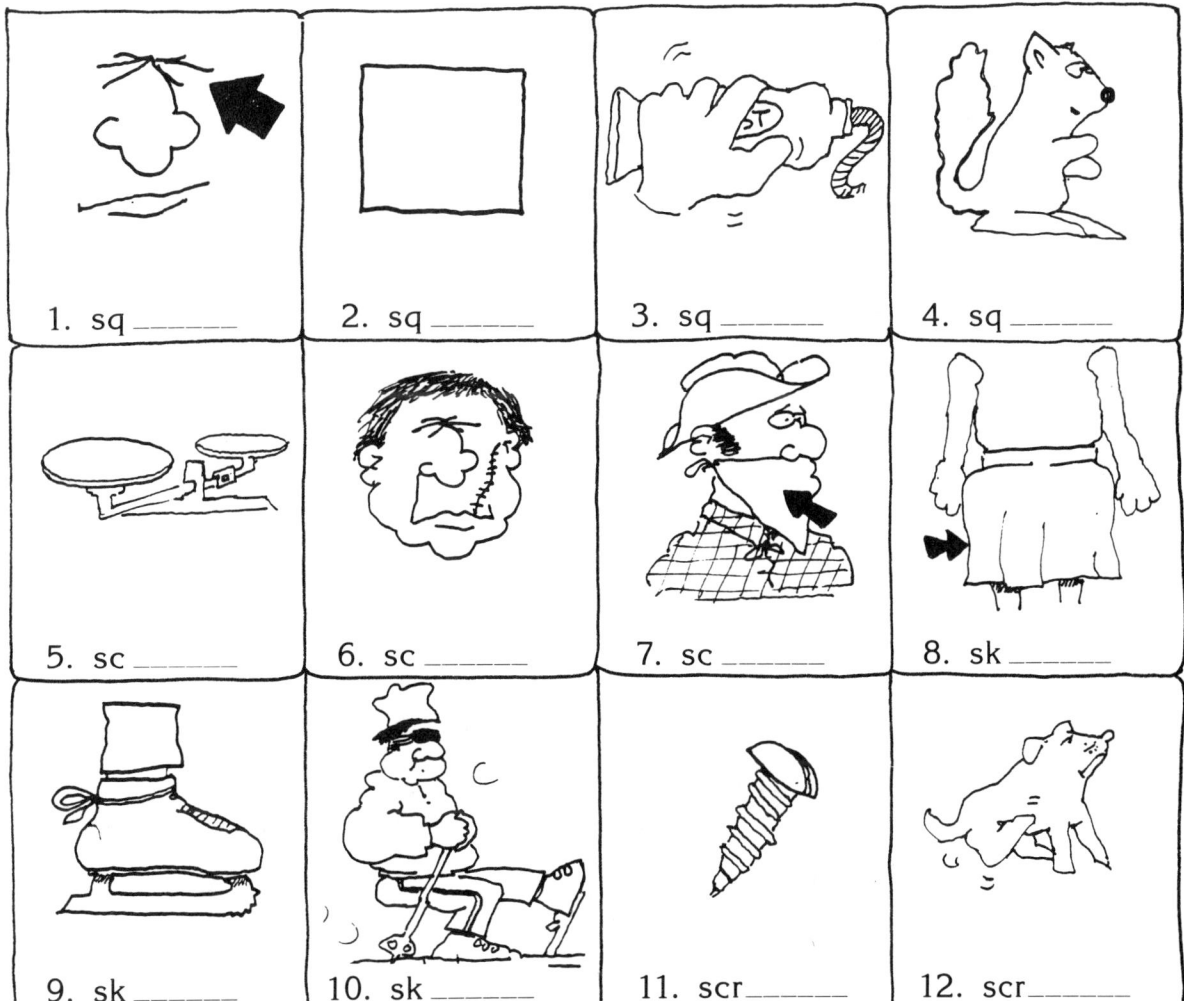

1. sq _____
2. sq _____
3. sq _____
4. sq _____
5. sc _____
6. sc _____
7. sc _____
8. sk _____
9. sk _____
10. sk _____
11. scr _____
12. scr _____

Read • Add   s

Kate	__ kate
key	__ ki
kin	__ kin
car	__ car
cool	__ chool
care	__ care
cream	__ cream

Listen • Write • Read

1. Can you ice _____?
2. A _____ has four sides.
3. _____ the lemons to make lemonade.
4. Fix the table with a _____.
5. Do you have a blue _____?
6. My _____ keeps my neck warm.
7. Do you like to water _____?
8. Dogs always _____ their fleas.

Review Vocabulary

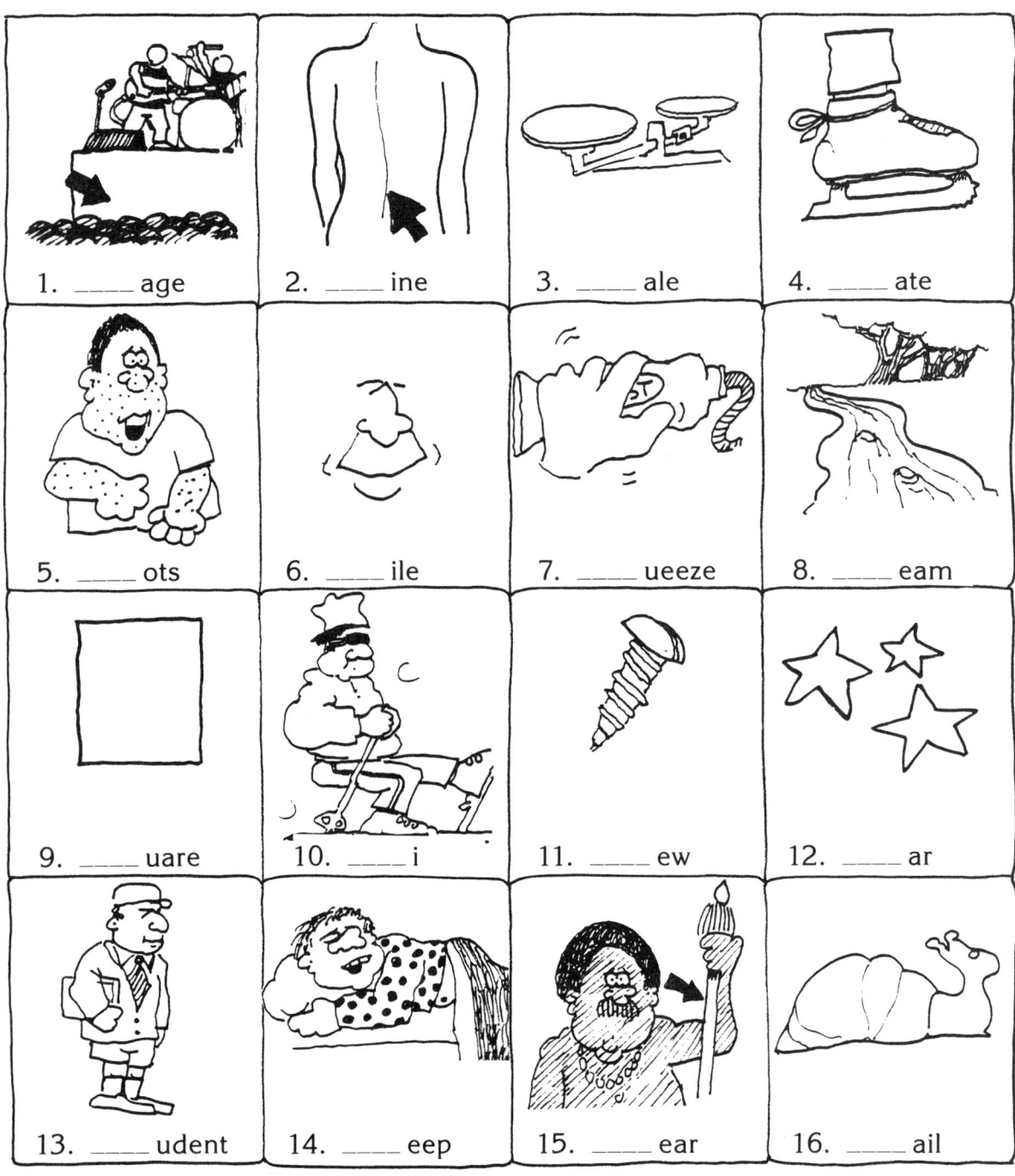

1. _____ age
2. _____ ine
3. _____ ale
4. _____ ate
5. _____ ots
6. _____ ile
7. _____ ueeze
8. _____ eam
9. _____ uare
10. _____ i
11. _____ ew
12. _____ ar
13. _____ udent
14. _____ eep
15. _____ ear
16. _____ ail

[š]–[šr]

Name it!

1. sh_____
2. sh_____
3. sh_____
4. sh_____
5. sh_____
6. shr_____
7. shr_____
8. shr_____

Read • Add __h__

sake	s __ ake
save	s __ ave
see	s __ e
sell	s __ ell
sip	s __ ip
sock	s __ ock
sore	s __ ore
sow	s __ ow

Read • Add __hr__

sink	s ____ ink
sign	s ____ ine
sub	s ____ ub
said	s ____ ed

Listen • Write • Read

1. Where is my other _____?
2. Are my green _____ dirty?
3. You have to _____ and _____!
4. Cotton _____ _____ sometimes.
5. Let's go to the _____.
6. Plant the _____ next to the house.
7. A _____ is a farm animal.
8. This _____ will go to Japan.

Review Vocabulary

page 34

Review Vocabulary

Review Vocabulary

Review Vocabulary

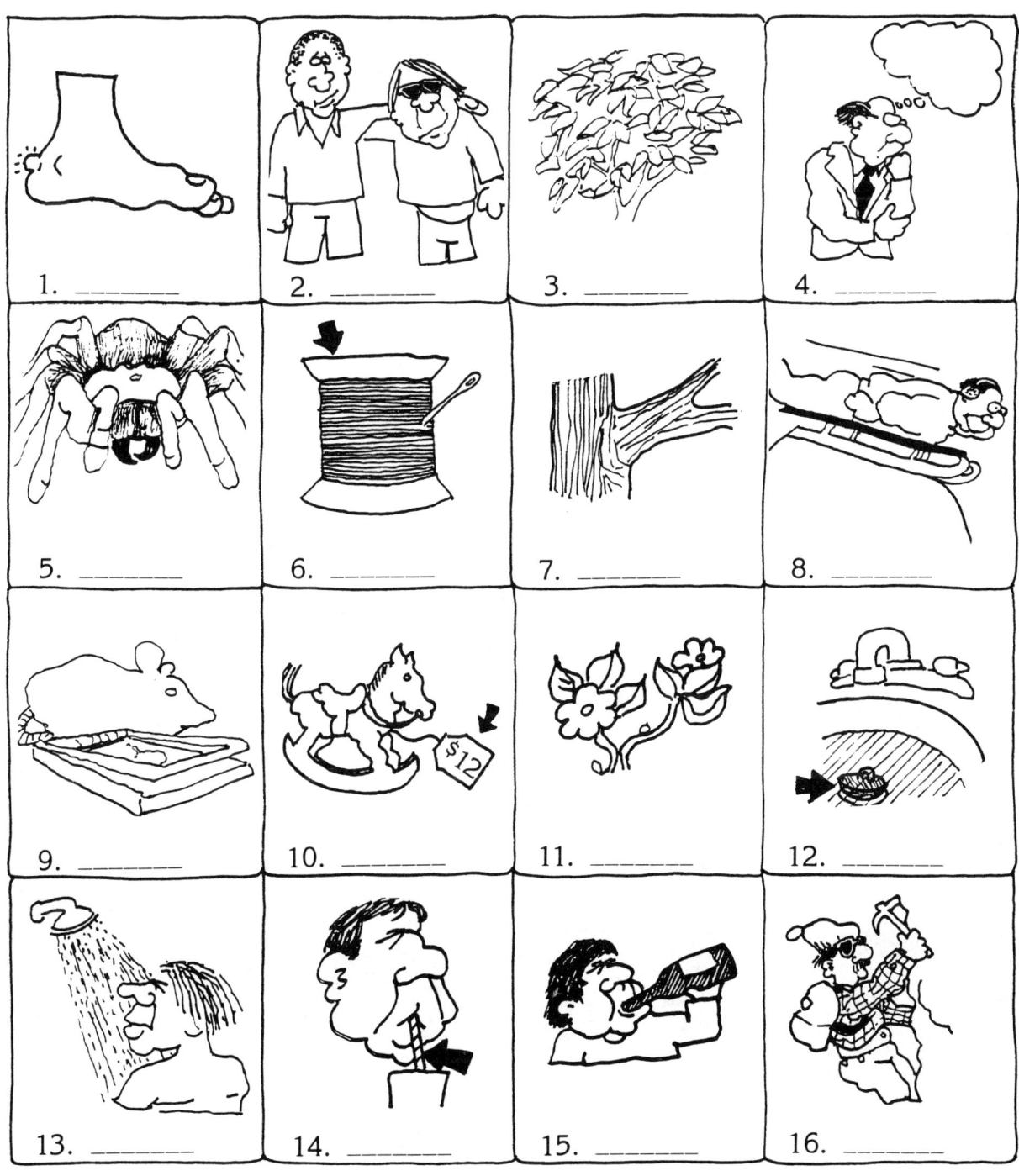

page 37

Review Vocabulary

Initial Clusters

Page 1
Name it!
1. block
2. blonde
3. blow
4. blind
5. blade
6. blister
7. bloom
8. blood

Listen • Write • Read
1. black
2. blimp
3. block
4. blow
5. bloom
6. blonde
7. blisters
8. blade

Page 2
Name it!
1. bracelet
2. braid
3. branch
4. brush
5. bread
6. bridge
7. broken
8. breakfast

Listen • Write • Read
1. brave
2. bright
3. broom
4. brush
5. branch
6. braid
7. bracelet
8. Bread

Page 3
Listen and Write
1. branch
2. blush
3. blue
4. bred
5. broom
6. blanch
7. brew
8. brush
9. bled
10. bloom
11. blade
12. braid

Listen and Write

1. bridge
2. brush
3. braid
4. blonde   brunette
5. branch   broken
6. blue   blanket

Page 4

Name it!

1. plug   2. plant   3. plume   4. plane
5. plow   6. plate   7. plump   8. play

Listen • Write • Read

1. play
2. plate
3. plump
4. please
5. plant
6. plume
7. plane
8. plug

Page 5

Name it!

1. price   2. prize   3. prince   4. present
5. print   6. prison   7. private   8. pray

Listen • Write • Read

1. present
2. private
3. prince
4. prison
5. print
6. pray
7. price
8. prize

Page 6

Listen and Write

1. plank
2. prow
3. pray
4. pleasant
5. plum
6. prank
7. present
8. plastic
9. problem
10. plow
11. practice
12. praise

Listen and Write

1. prunes   plums
2. play
3. practice
4. plastic
5. plow
6. Please

Page 7   Review Vocabulary

1. bracelet
2. prize
3. blade
4. plug
5. blister
6. plant
7. prince
8. braid
9. price
10. branch
11. bloom
12. prison
13. bridge
14. plume
15. print
16. blood

Page 8

Name it!

1. clover
2. closet
3. clock
4. clamp
5. cliff
6. clothes
7. clip
8. climb

Listen • Write • Read

1. clothes
2. closet
3. clover
4. cliff
5. clock
6. climb
7. clip
8. clamp

Page 9

Name it!

1. cricket 2. crown 3. cross 4. crayon
5. crib 6. crook 7. crab 8. cry

Listen • Write • Read

1. cry
2. crown
3. crayons
4. crab
5. cricket
6. crib
7. crook
8. Cross

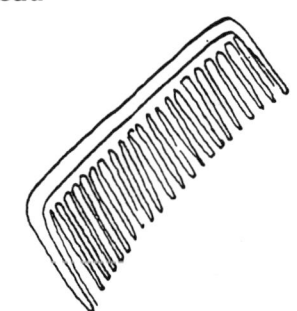

Page 10

Listen and Write

1. crack 5. crash 9. crowds
2. claw 6. clack 10. clash
3. class 7. clouds 11. claw
4. crock 8. crass 12. clock

Listen and Write

1. class
2. crowd
3. clouds
4. claws
5. crash
6. clamp

Page 11

Name it!

1. glass 2. globe 3. glove 4. glue

Listen • Write • Read

1. gloves
2. glad
3. glass
4. globe
5. glance
6. gloss
7. glue
8. glaze

Page 12

Name it!

1. grapes
2. grandmother
3. grass
4. grain
5. grin
6. groom
7. gray
8. grow

Listen • Write • Read

1. grin
2. grass
3. grain
4. groom
5. Grapes
6. grow
7. grandmother
8. gray

Page 13

Listen and Write

1. grass
2. gloom
3. glue
4. gleam
5. graze
6. grade
7. groom
8. green
9. gloss
10. grew
11. glass
12. glaze

Listen and Write

1. grow
2. glue
3. grass   green
4. glass
5. grill
6. grade

Page 14

1. glue
2. cry
3. cricket
4. clamp
5. clover
6. crown
7. grandma
8. globe
9. grass
10. closet
11. cross
12. grain
13. crayon
14. glass
15. grin
16. cliff

Page 15   Review Vocabulary

Listen and Write

1. broom
2. crack
3. play
4. glint
5. brown
6. plan
7. crush
8. greed
9. plush
10. gloom
11. clay
12. bran
13. blush
14. print
15. bloom
16. black
17. crown
18. clack
19. plate
20. breed
21. clown
22. groom
23. brush
24. gray

Name it!

1. present
2. crib
3. block
4. clock
5. grapes
6. brush
7. glove
8. plane

Page 16

Name it!

1. flag
2. flame
3. flashlight
4. flea
5. flock
6. flood
7. flowers
8. flute

Listen • Read • Write

1. flag
2. flame
3. flashlight
4. flea
5. flowers
6. flake
7. flute
8. flock

Page 17

Name it!

1. frog
2. fruit
3. frame
4. frying pan
5. France
6. freckles
7. free
8. friend

Listen • Read • Write

1. frying pan
2. friends
3. freckles
4. France

5. fruit
6. frog
7. free
8. frame

Page 18

Listen and Write

1. fresh
2. flank
3. fright
4. fruit
5. flame
6. flight
7. flesh
8. freezer
9. frank
10. flute
11. freight
12. front

Listen and Write

1. fresh
2. fruit
3. freezer
4. flute
5. front
6. free

Page 19

Name it!

1. train
2. tray
3. trunk
4. tree
5. trumpet
6. trail
7. truck
8. trap

Listen • Write • Read

1. tree
2. truck
3. train
4. tray
5. trap
6. trunk
7. Trumpets
8. trail

Page 20

Name it!

1. drum
2. drapes
3. drive
4. drugs
5. drink
6. dress
7. dream
8. drain

Listen • Write • Read

1. dress
2. drink
3. drum
4. dream
5. drug
6. drive
7. Drapes
8. drain

Page 21

Listen and Write

1. trail
2. truck
3. dry
4. tree
5. dress
6. true
7. try
8. drop
9. trip
10. drip
11. drink
12. drapes

Listen • Write • Read

1. tree
2. drive
3. train
4. Dry
5. dress
6. draw

truck

Page 22

Name it!

1. fruit
2. trunk
3. French
4. trap
5. free
6. flood
7. trail
8. friends
9. trumpet
10. tree
11. freckles
12. flea
13. flashlight
14. dream
15. truck
16. drug

Page 23

Name it!

1. thin
2. thief
3. thank you
4. think
5. three
6. throat
7. throw
8. thread

Listen and Write

1. thread
2. thin
3. three
4. think

5. Thank
6. Throw
7. throat
8. thief

Page 24

Listen and Write

1. train
2. friends
3. flame
4. drum
5. thin
6. truck
7. frog
8. thread
9. true
10. draw
11. think
12. fruit
13. truck
14. flute
15. drink
16. throat
17. three
18. flag
19. tray
20. frame
21. dresser
22. drip
23. fly
24. thief

Name it!

1. train
2. flag
3. dress
4. frog
5. thin
6. throat
7. flower
8. frame

Page 25   Review Vocabulary

1. private
2. plate
3. blonde
4. clothes
5. tray
6. gray
7. frying pan
8. crab
9. drive
10. blind
11. pray
12. drum
13. groom
14. clip
15. drain
16. crook

Page 26

Name it!

1. spool
2. spider
3. sports
4. spill
5. spade
6. spots
7. spear
8. spine
9. spring
10. spray
11. splash
12. split

Listen • Write • Read

1. spool
2. sports
3. spiders
4. spill
5. Spray
6. splash
7. spots
8. spend

Page 27

Name it!

1. stove
2. student
3. stamp
4. stomach
5. steam
6. stage
7. stars
8. strike
9. straw
10. stripes
11. string
12. street

Listen • Write • Read

1. stamp
2. stream
3. stomach
4. string
5. stars
6. steam
7. student
8. stand   stage

Page 28

Name it!

1. smile
2. smoke
3. small
4. smell
5. snake
6. sneeze
7. snore
8. snail
9. slow
10. slide
11. sled
12. sleep

Listen • Write • Read

1. smell   smoke
2. snail   slow
3. snore
4. Smile
5. small
6. slide
7. snake
8. sneeze

Page 29

Listen • Write • Read

1. speak
2. spray
3. sting
4. small
5. string
6. straw
7. snow
8. slow
9. stay
10. snake

Page 30 Review Vocabulary S-clusters

1. spool
2. small
3. stamp
4. straw
5. strike
6. spring
7. snore
8. sports
9. string
10. splash
11. slow
12. smoke
13. snake
14. sneeze
15. stove
16. spray

Page 31

1. squint
2. square
3. squeeze
4. squirrel
5. scale
6. scar
7. scarf
8. skirt
9. skate
10. ski
11. screw
12. scratch

Listen • Write • Read

1. skate
2. square
3. Squeeze
4. screw
5. skirt
6. scarf
7. ski
8. scratch

Page 32 Review Vocabulary S-clusters

1. stage
2. spine
3. scale
4. skate
5. spots
6. smile
7. squeeze
8. stream
9. square
10. ski
11. screw
12. stars
13. student
14. sleep
15. spear
16. snail

Page 33

Name it!

1. shoe
2. sheep
3. ship
4. shower
5. shave
6. shrimp
7. shrub
8. shrink

Listen • Write • Read

1. shoe
2. socks
3. shave   shower
4. socks   shrink
5. show
6. shrub
7. sheep
8. ship

Page 34   Review Vocabulary

1. scarf
2. bracelet
3. blow
4. think
5. grandma
6. stomach
7. block
8. shave
9. cry
10. drape
11. drink
12. steam
13. slide
14. drain
15. braid
16. blond

Page 35   Review Vocabulary

1. shoe
2. dream
3. spill
4. print
5. plane
6. shower
7. small
8. blood
9. scar
10. thief
11. thank you
12. grass
13. blow
14. brush
15. trumpet
16. squirrel

Page 36   Review Vocabulary

1. spade
2. blade
3. blind
4. globe
5. squeeze
6. flock
7. clip
8. three
9. prize
10. freckles
11. thank you
12. grape
13. smell
14. cricket
15. pray
16. ship

Page 37   Review Vocabulary

1. blister
2. friends
3. shrub
4. think
5. spider
6. spool
7. branch
8. sled
9. trap
10. price
11. bloom
12. plug
13. shower
14. straw
15. drink
16. climb

Page 38   Review Vocabulary

1. prison
2. string
3. plant
4. scale
5. smoke
6. crib
7. shoe
8. glue
9. present
10. screw
11. shrink
12. French
13. drive
14. clothes
15. free
16. bridge